T0105568

REFLECTION UPON A WORLD

SQUIRREL

authorHOUSE®

AuthorHouse™
1663 Liberty Drive
Bloomington, IN 47403
www.authorhouse.com
Phone: 1-800-839-8640

First published by AuthorHouse 12/21/2010

ISBN: 978-1-4520-8274-5 (e)
ISBN: 978-1-4520-8273-8 (sc)

Library of Congress Control Number: 2010918969

Printed in the United States of America

This book is printed on acid-free paper.

Certain stock imagery © Thinkstock.

Introduction

A Collection of poems; written from the soul of a man celebrating life, family, and friends. Poems that give thanks to God for all that he has done and has given to the world.

Poems that challenge one to look at self and ask some tough questions; "Who Am I", what are my values, and where am I headed.

Celebrate and remember those who have touched our lives, poems. Remember and reflex on loved ones no longer with us, poems. Family, friends, and love ones that will never be forgotten.

Reflection upon a world; sit back, relax and open your mind, and the poems will touch your heart and refresh your soul.

Table of Contents

Section 4 – Where Am I?   **39**

Section 5 – Friends And Special Someone   **63**

Section One

Faith, Hope, & Love

Value of Friendship

A Teacher, Prophet, Parent
Said to his
Student, Disciple, Child
You are my **Friend!**

Who Am I?

Who Am I?
I ask as I sit in front of the mirror
I review the past
Every goal I reached and didn't reach
I ask the same question, who Am I?

As I strive to succeed in the game of life
Family and friends alike give me a pat on the back
The world looks and sees success and failure in their terms
Still I ponder,
Who Am I?

I set new goals, new values, and new roads to travel
Success builds upon success
Failure is just a tool to learn from
Yet, the question persists,
Who Am I?

Then in the still of the night
In the calm of the storm
The answer to the question
Who am I?
I am,
A child of God!!!

Someone knocking at my door

Someone knocking at my door
But I have no time to answer
So I hurry on my way.

Someone knocking at my door
I see no one through the glass in the door
Now I'm too afraid to open the door.

Someone knocking at my door
But I think it's the television
So I continue to watch.
The knocking persists, yet I'm unaware.
So active is my imagination that I'm hearing things.

Someone knocking at my door
But I'm not expecting company,
So I send the visitor on his way.

Someone knocking at my door
As I open the door
It is Jesus knocking at the door -
The door of my heart!

In a Moment

It takes just a moment.

From seconds to days
From days to years,
Maybe even a life time
To reach that moment.

But, in that moment
Life is renewed.
Life has new purpose.
Eyes are sharper.
Ears are keener
Voices are clearer.

In that moment,
The world is less confusing.
Goals are more focused.
The missions are more attainable.

In that moment,
The heart rejoices.
Friends are happier.
Love one's cry.
Love is the order of life.

In that moment,
I said yes to the Lord
And he gave me life.

Gift from God

A gift from God, that last a life time.
A gift from God that no other can compare
A gift so precious, that science is trying to duplicate.

A gift so special it makes the proud humble.
A gift so special it makes the strong cry.

A gift from God that repairs the broken hearted
A gift so special, that it removes tears.

A gift from God, which is a joy to all.
A gift from God, which keeps giving.
God's gift, A child name Jesus!

Goal of Life?

What is the goal of life?
Is it to collect riches?
Is it to attain fame?
Is it to play to show others that you were here?

Generations have passed, yet the game continues.
Family members remember family members,
But for how long?

What does tomorrow hold?
What does today show?
Death comes to us all.
But life only to God's children!

Questions of Hope

My God why have you forsaken me?
My foes stands poised to strike
My friends stand idly by
My family questions, what have you done?

I ask for thy help,
But my prayers go unanswered.

As my foes strike,
My help arrives, for I kept my faith.
Reward is at hand.
I'm in the presence of God.

Crimes of Life

My crimes are countless.
So many I care not to remember.

I go before the judge daily.
Yet, he is compassionate to me every time.

The State seeks to condemn
My lawyer knows all.
Angels and Saints fill my defense team.

Before the judge, I enter my plea.
Forgive me Father, for I have Sinned.

The Fury of Man

Patience has run thin,
Nerves on edge,
The breaking point is near,
The smallest thing will cause a chain reaction.

Compassion is limited.
Wisdom replaced by illogic,
No longer can I stand idly by.

The world is about to feel my raft.
The wrong word has been spoken,
The wrong actions have been taken.
Anger has replaced reason,
The mind prepares for attack,
Revenge is the only thought.

The hour is at hand,
Stand back friends,
None can withstand my fury.

There will be no mercy,
For none was given.

The door of my fury is open!

Wait!
There is a cross in the path!

Wisdom returns,
Anger subsides,
Forgiveness is back.

RELIEF

The Sun
Offers no relief,
No comfort.

The Moon
Turns Day to Night
Re-enforces what is known.

Tears flow freely
Only God knows how many.

The Waiting…
Seconds to Hours
Hours to Years
How long must I wait?

For the Sweet Scent of Yesterday
Has turned Sour Today.

For in the End,
My relief has always been Near
But I was too Blind to see,
That the Spirit was with me!

Run Silent Run Deep

Words trapped within
None need to be spoken

Silent, Let Wisdom
Run its course
Deep within
Free to move about

Think, Think
For Wisdom has been granted.

Run Silent, Run Deep

From Jesus to Moses to Jesus
The lessons are visible

Run Silent, Run Deep

For their one can communicate with God in Peace.

The Promise

High above
Sea below
Air in-between
I'm with you.

To the left
To the right
In the front
In the back
I'm with you.

Listen
See
Feel
The presence of Jesus!

The Smallest Pieces

What is one grain of Sand?
Compared to the Desert?

What is one drop of Water?
Compared to the Ocean?

What is one Star?
Compared to the Universe?

What is one Soul?
Compared to the Human race?

All are parts of a greater whole.
All are important.
All are special to God!

Never Alone

Day turns to night
Night turns to day
No one calls
No one answers the pages
Message after message goes unanswered
Wonderment, what has happen?
Never Alone.

Surrounded by four walls
Night after night
Day after day
No one to talk to
No one to listen
Never Alone.

No sounds of joy
Sounds of tears fill the room
No laughter
No children playing
A house so quiet
A pin echoes loudly during the day
Never Alone.

Walk the grounds
No neighbor seen
No neighbor heard
Never Alone.

From birth until death
Second to second
Never Alone.

Avoided by family
Stranded by friends
Ignored by strangers
Isolated by coworkers
Never Alone.

For the Angels provide protection
The Saints pray.
And Jesus always by thy side!

War of Wars

It was a battle like no other,
It was the ultimate battle
The winner dispatches the loser
Now the loser sets new sights
New goals,
Destruction is that goal.

It's a new day.
The battle rages on,
It has been fought for countless generations.

The prize is precious to all,
So special is the prize,
Combat is fought soldier to soldier,
Hand to hand.
There is no lack of commitment on both sides.

The battle rages on
When will it end?

The prize is worth the battle.
The prize,
Soul of Man!

Condemned

Condemned
By jury of Peers
Yet who is my Equal?

Condemned
Guilty beyond doubt
Threat to the powerful.
Threat to the leaders.

Condemned
The Judge…
Knows I was framed
Fear…
For Life and Limb
Fear…
Give the people what they want.

Condemned
Witnesses…
The prosecution pays
Witnesses…
Their stories contradict

Condemned
Fear…
Weakness of Jury…
Fear…
Motivated…

Condemned
Forman…
The Verdict…
We the Jury…
Crucify Him!!!
Crucify Him!!!
Crucify Him!!!

Section Two

REMEMBER

. . .

Goodbye

Dust Settles
Body at Rest

Dreams
Now
Memories

Family;
Friends;

Good times
Bad Times

Tears filled with Joy
Tears…

Remember …

The Light

Peace

Goodbye,
Until we meet again!

Rest in Peace

Death
Cold chill
Stills the Body

Warm Memories
Refreshes the Soul

Water forms
Where the Eye rest

Death Knocked
Friend Answered

The Soul
Goes
The Body Stays

Death
Is the End
And
The Beginning

Death
Never Separate those in our Heart

Fallen Heroes

They were special from birth
To help others was their mission
A goal worthy of the Saints

In grammar school they were crossing guards.
In high school they were on school patrol.

Few remember them
Victims thank them
Criminals curse them.

It's not for praise, nor glory
It's just for the common good
For the love of life and happiness of others.

Then one day in the heat of a battle
A hero has fallen.

For a moment we cry
For a day we morn
Many will forget them
Few will remember them
To all the fallen heroes
Rest in Peace.

Farewell to a Good Samaritan

For two years we served together
Patrolling the hallways of Westinghouse High.

Defending student and school.
Running to emergencies without a care.
Throwing safety to the wind,
Two children without fear,
Courage our only weapon.
For this we graduated with honors.

The desire to help others burned deep within my friend
Then one day in a Brooklyn train station,
Running to the aid of a stranger,
His courage was not enough,
A Good Samaritan has fallen.

A family cries,
Friends wonder why.
To the end we say,
Malcolm Brown,
Rest in Peace.

Section Three

Emotion

Depression and Disappointment

Depression and disappointment are the same this day.
The mind wants what it cannot deliver
Dreams have betrayed me
I long for what I do not want.

Depression and disappointment are the same this day
The seed of the world has taken root in my mind
Madison Avenue has corrupted my dreams
Dreams; All day I dream about what I want but cannot have.

Depression and disappointment are the same this day.
The will is weak
The soul is cold
The wants are filled
But depression and disappointments are still there.

I seek help, but no one understands
The struggles and pains are mine alone
I turn to the source of all.

Depression and disappointment are gone this day.
God helps all.

Depression

Heavy is the heart
Trouble is the soul
Depression is the order of the day.

Peace cannot be found at home or away
Success escapes thee
Family evades thee
Depression is served daily.

Friends mock thee
Strangers question thee
One doubts thou every move
Depression is thou companion.

Failure is thou middle name
Last place is just a dream
To finish is the goal
Depression is the norm.

Wonderment begins
As the body begins to fail
Thou eyes see no longer
Thou ears do not hear
Depression temps the soul.

Troubles Go Away

Another day dawns
The troubles of yesterday
Will not PASS.

How I wish I could
Sleep the day away.

I dream,
I pray,
For help this day.

Then the Angels arrived,
Michael, Gabriel,
And a thousand more.

Standing by my side
I face the troubles of the day.
Oh, what a difference a prayer makes.

Nature's Ways

How calm is the morning?
Listening to the rain,
Gently tapping against the window pane.

How tranquil the day.
So calming,
So relaxing,
One can sleep all day.

How peaceful to know,
Nature cares so much.

Listen

Listen to the birds
Singing a song.

Listen to the ocean,
Wave after wave,
Pushing against the shore.

Listen to the wind
Whispering as it moves
From tree to tree
Building to building.

Listen to the morning
As the fog rolls away.

Listen to the day
Quiet as it may be.

Listen to the night
As the creatures scurry to shelter.

Listen and hear,
God talking.

Slow Down For A Moment

STOP!!!!

From your busy day.
Remove thoughts of the task at hand.

Clear your mind.

Look at the world,
See the beauty,
Smell the roses,
Feel the warmth of the Sun,
Listen to the sounds of nature,
Taste the daily bread,
Marvel at what has been given.
Don't let life pass you by.

For the day only last but a few hours.
It would be a shame,
To miss this day!

Silence in the Night

Silence in the night,
The moonlight breaks through the cracks in the shades.
The wind howls gently against the window panes.
The body relaxes in the comfort of the chair.
The mind unwinds from the pressures of the day.

Silence in the night,
Calm overcomes the soul.
Reflections of the day are put away
Troubles of tomorrow are for another moment

Silence in the night,
Drifting deeper and deeper into the calm of the night.
The wind whispers like a parent talking to a child
Relax, relax, all is well this night.

Silence in the night,
Slowly the body shift into a more comfortable position.
Dreams, sweet dreams fills the mind.
All is well.
Life is refreshing.

Silence in the night,
Good night....

Soldier's Moment

The Wind quietly whispers Taps.

The Mind,
Drifts
Deeper and deeper
Into Silence,
Slowly loosing
Conscience of
Time and space.

Drifting deeper,
Ever so deeper
Where memories Dwell.
Good times
Hilarious times
Special times

Drifting…
Deeper and deeper
Without Aids
Without Cares
With Smiles!

Drifting…
Into Subconscious
Where Dreams Reside.
Where
What Ifs…
Are the order of the Day.
Fame,
Fortune,
Happiness
Are Guaranteed.

The Mind,
Drifting…
Drifting
Deeper and deeper
Into Peace
Into Utopia!

IN COMING!
IN COMING!

Quiet Times
Shattered!
The Battle rages!

Tension of the Day

The arrows are in the bows,
The swords are out of their shafts,
Guns are visible,
Weapons of destruction are ready,
The state of war is constant.

Walk lightly,
Listen intently.
The fuses are lit,
Tension is high,
Nerves are frail,
This is a Red Alert!

This is a battle zone
Nowhere to run,
Nowhere to hide,
Condition Red, Red Alert!

This is life,
In the big city.

Potential

In the silence
In the empty spaces
Questions arise
What has happened?

Success seemed so certain
Potential so great
Life had so much promise
Now I question
What has happened?

Sun shined so bright
Moon glowed so radiantly
Stars filled the sky
Now I question
What has happened?

Life was a dream,
Dreams coming true
Ideas filled the mind.
Praises came from one and all
Now I question
What has happened?

As night turns to day
It's time to start anew
The past is gone
Today gives renewed hope,
To reach my potential.

BLESSING

A Smile
That Stretches from Ear to Ear

A Smile
Enlightening a gloomy Day

A Smile
That Shines as the Sun

A Smile
Radiant as the Moon

A Smile
Calming as the Setting Sun

A Smile
For all the world to See

From Day to Night
Night to Day
Keep on Smiling
For you are Blessed!

Good Morning

The Dawn of a new day
The rising of the morning Sun
Life gives another chance.

New hopes,
New dreams,
All starts fresh,
The day's promises so great,
What a difference from yesterday.

Smell the air,
Admire the fog burn away.
A world to explore
So much to do,
So much to see,
So little time,
For the day is six hours old.

Look out world
For here I come
Eager to learn,
Willing to help
Happy just to be.
But first I pray,
Giving thanks for another Day!

Section Four

Where Am I ?

My Foe

My foe evades my every move.
My foe strikes with the skill of a surgeon
And the precision of a laser.
My foe attacks at will and without mercy.

Yes, this foe knows my every move.
My foe is greater than I.
My foe makes me look bad before God and family alike.

I seek to identify this foe
This foe hides within the shadows at night
This foe blends with the light during the day.

Finally, after years of searching
I know who this foe is.
To my surprise,
I have always known my greatest foe
The foe is
Me!

THE EGO

Thou Ego stands in the way
It changes the simplest of wants
Into the greatest of needs.

Thou Ego
Pushes Man to great heights.

Thou Ego
Strips a friend of their worth.

The Ego of the Human Being,
Part of who we are.

Do not let your Ego,
Keep your Soul from God!

Compassion

Its war now; with no end in sight
It started so simply
A disagreement that is trivial in nature.

Compassion was replaced by fear,
The fear of showing weakness
Not even the diplomats could stop it.

Compassion replaced by ignorance.
The bluffs did not work,
Iron hands were met by iron hands
The wills would not bend.

It's all out war.
Both sides did not want war.
Both sides refused to talk.
Both sides too scared to talk.

Compassion is gone!
Today a mother cries,
A father angrier
Because their child will not be coming home
Where is the compassion for them?

The Lost Art

Compassion
How you ask
For what you do not give.

Compassion
A virtue all too forgotten.

Compassion
Limitless in scope,
Endless in grace.

Compassion
A two way street,
Often running One way

Compassion
Ask only for what
You are willing to give!

Self-Centered

Your words have fallen on deaf ears
Your stories are of no interest.
Your praises only satisfy your needs.

Heed my words
For the time is coming
When you will understand how shallow
Your words are.

How thoughtless your deeds
Stop seeking praises
Stop patting yourself on the back.

The time is near
When the truth will be revealed.
But how I feel for you,
Because you still will not understand.

Open your heart,
Free your mind,
Then you will understand
The truth of the messenger!

Politics

Words fall short of their goal
Actions support not the words
That's politics.

Expectations without facts
Dreams, visions, images
Coated with sugar.
Sweet to the mind,
Dangerous to the body.
That's politics.

Facts cloud wishes.
Hope planted by words of enthusiasm.
Promises supported by space.
Form without substance.
That's politics.

The Elevator

The doors open, but no one moves.
Tension builds
The doors begin to close
The stares are intense,
Like Lions stalking their prey.

The stares are deadly,
Gabriel stands before me.
Tension mounting
Teeth begin to grind
Throats are clearing
Fists are tightening.

The air thickens
The tension is boiling
The silence is unnerving
Then, the silence is broken;

I'm sorry, I pressed the wrong floor.
Now there is laughter.

The Truth

The Truth
A dual edge sword
Both Sweet and Sour

Sour to the Mind
Sweet for the Soul

The Truth Hurts
Yet, there is no pain like a Lie

Especially...
When the One who is Deceived,
Is Self!

To Be the Best

To be the best
Is a lifelong quest.
Day to day
Moment to moment
Strive to be the best.

No mountain too high to climb,
No ocean too deep to swim,
Day and night, night and day,
To be the best is the quest.

Not to be the best runner.
Not to be the fastest swimmer.
Not even to be the best boxer.
But still strive to be the best.

Not the smartest person,
Not the best singer,
Still strive to be the Best.

One day you will be the best,
The best that you can be!

FORGIVENESS

Words cannot express.
Action offers insight.

Is it an Art?
Is it Grace?

If the Heart cannot Forgive,
How can the Mind?

How often we Ask
For what we cannot Give?

Compassion and Forgiveness
Start in the Heart

For there Lies the
True value of Man

The KING

To be the Ruler
The king of the Castle

Constantly on Guard
No Time,
To Rest
To enjoy the Fruits of the Kingdom.

Enemies encamped around thou Kingdom,
Waiting to Strike

Enemies, hidden in the Shadows,
The Shadows of Friendship.
How well did Cesar Learn
The enemy within.

Stand tall,
Stand proud

For there is no turning back
For in the end,
All Rulers must face
The King!!!

Today

Hundreds are Born
Thousands Die

Today's Sorrow
Is Yesterday's Joy
Is Tomorrow's Anger

To Please Some
Others must Die.

All this Started
Because,
I wanted to Rule
Today!

The Game

Game full of promise.
Each player with our own vision, dreams, and rainbows.

Trying, striving, and working toward that silver lining.
For some,
The road travels through Fame and fortune'
For others, Poverty and despair.

Someday we all reach that silver lining.
Then the question is asked,
Did you play by the <u>Ten</u> rules of the game?

Saddest Words

For years I lived my own way
Not worried about others,
Living only to fulfill my own needs and desires.

Good and evil did not matter.
The only laws I obeyed were my own.
I lived by the sword.
Money was my king.
Lies were the way of life.

Friends mattered not.
Family members I used.
I spoke harsh words to one and all.

Now it's judgment time.
God has spoken the saddest words.
Child, prepare for Satan and his angels.

Saddest Words to be Heard

I lived my own way!
Not worried about others.

Living to fulfill my own needs and desires
Good and evil were irrelevant
I lived by the sword
I defended by the Gun

Lies were the way of my life
I spoke harsh words to one and all

Now that it's judgment time,
God has spoken …
Child; prepare for Satan and his angles.

Testimony From One of the Boyz

I Lived *Fast.*

I Lived **Large.**

I played **HARD.**

I Died *Young.*

For a Moment…
I was the <u>MAN</u>!

My name,
Respected and FEARED!

I RULED,
the *Corner, the Block, the Hood!*

But now, I'm fuel
For the ***FIRE!***

The Trap

A World
Three blocks long

Money flowing…
Grants and Benjamin
Stacked to the ceiling

Fame and Glory
A legend in my own time

Woman and Champagne
Party hard
Party long

Today I live
For there is no tomorrow

Trap… Trap
Between
The Police and Judas

Each trying to end my Rule

Living Fast
Will I make 25?

Trap…
Trap…
In the world of
Cocaine!

The Bullet

The Bullet
No one Heard
No one Seen

Steel
Meets
Flesh

Millimeters
Versus
Seven Layers of Skin

Blood
Meets
Air

Heart Pumps…
No More.

Soul
Embraces
The Light

The Bullet
Resides
Where
I'm no more.

The Bullet
Justice,
Will the two ever Meet?

Waiting for Tomorrow

Tomorrow is but a day away.
So many promises start tomorrow,
So many dreams begin tomorrow,
Tomorrow is another day.

Many deeds await tomorrow
Tomorrow is but a whisper away.

New roads to travel,
New friends to meet,
New life to lead,
Oh, how I'll wait for tomorrow.

New day dawn
But tomorrow is still a day away.

Postpone till tomorrow,
For today is too busy.

Tomorrow will have time for many things.
Some small, some tall, and some great,
Oh, how I dream about tomorrow.

No mountain too high,
No road too small,
Tomorrow is a new lease on life.

But today is the day,
The Lord has called.
Tomorrow is no more
Dreams of change come to an end,
Promises to self cannot be kept.

Now the Heaven's ponder
What I wonder,
Was today good enough?

The Price of Life

What is Gold?
That some value
It more than life?

What is Silver?
That some value
It more than helping a neighbor?

What is Bronze?
That some would
Steal to acquire?

Have the Metals
Become more valuable than
The Man?

For a bar of Gold,
I am no more.

Is acquiring the Metals,
For storage
Worth the Price?

What is the value of Gold?
When God calls?

Words of Truth

Words without interest,
Stories with no meaning,
What do you want from me?

Ask me not to give praises,
Ask me not to lie.
For the truth I speak,
The truth you do not want to hear.

But in the end,
Only the truth will free you.

Friendly Fire

It made contact at the speed of sound.
It did more damage than any bullet.
Yet, it left no visible marks.

It robbed the heart of its compassion.
It made the senses numb,
The body is stung.

It prompts the mind to seek revenge
Yet, for this attack there is no revenge
For the attacker is a friend.

Toward this friend, there is no anger
This friend understands not the power of their weapon.
The weapon was fired without forethought.
A weapon too readily available to all,
The weapon, a word!!

Friends No More

To be such good friends
Now we barely speak.

The smiles are gone,
We look at each other with anger.
The handshakes are firm but competitive.
We talk about each other
No longer are we friends.

We treat each other worse than enemies.
We despise the ground the other walks.

What happened to forgive and forget?
What happened to friends to the end?
Was it money?
Was it work related?
Was it a sporting game?
Was it something said?

Whatever the cause
We are friends no more!
All I ask is why?

Section Five

Friends
And
Special Someone

Friends

We stand side by side
Toe to toe
We are friends.

We share,
We care
We are friends.

We compete not
We compare not
For we are friends.

Time passes
Distance changes
Still we are friends.

Time improves what is
No words can say
Thanks for being a friend.

A Thought Away

In seconds we became friends
A bond that transcends time

In a crowd
In the car
You're only a thought away.

Bad or good day,
Calm or busy day,
Rainy or sunny day,
You're only a thought away.

We may not see each other,
We may not hear from each other,
Yet, you are only a thought away.

Thousand miles or ten feet,
Thoughts bring you near.
Remember today and every day
You are only a thought away.

Memories

Time moves along
Memories remain
Pictures of the past
Bring tears in the present.

Friends have come
Friends have gone
Oh how I miss my friends.

From kindergarten
To college
Friendships last forever.

We have grown together
Now we have grown apart
Yet, we will always be friends!

Day Dreaming

The body is at rest
The mind begins to drift
The trouble of the day gives way.

The mind begins to wonder
What is for dinner?

Relaxation is at hand
Slowly the mind drifts
Forgotten friends come to mind
I wonder how ... is doing?

The wonderment turns to joy.
Remembering fun of old
Slowly a smile surfaces upon your face
Even a smirk or two.

As the mind drifts even deeper
A conversation begins
Remember when we did...
Now a smile covers the whole face
Laughter is heard.

Suddenly; the mind drifts no more.
The trip down memory lane is over.
The commercial has ended.
Now back to the show.

The Flower

The Flower
Seed Planted by Nature
Blossom to Beauty

The Flower
Treasured by One
Adored by Many
Admired by All

The Flower
Beauty that is Breathless
Beauty that is Speechless
Beauty that is Endless

The Flower's
Aroma
Fills the Air
Calms the Soul

The Flower
Brings Peace
Where there is Stress

The Flower
Is,
You!

Thanks

Today I give thanks,
For I have seen beauty.

Forgive me as I stare,
For none can compare,
To your beauty
I wish not to possess your beauty,
But admire.

I see the wear of the day upon your eyes.
I see your tired reflexes as you wait for your ride.
Yet, your beauty is one to remember.

I do not know your name,
But I will always remember you.

From today until the end of time,
All will be compared to you.

Now I give thanks to God,
My eyes have seen what many long to see.
Today,
I have seen beauty!

Waiting for the Words

I have watched from afar,
I have admired your beauty.
Even more I admire what cannot be seen but only felt,
The beauty of a kind soul.

For countless days I have searched for words,
For deeds of grandeur,
For adventure to impress
Yet none seems worthy.

Now all I can do is wait
For words,
Both kind and comforting,
For expressions,
Pleasing and unthreatening,
Not knowing whether the waiting is right or wrong,
Knowing that I may not have another chance to speak,
Believing that one day I will call you friend.

Until that day,
I offer these simple unspoken words,
Have a nice Day!!!

Definition of Love

How *D*eep is our Love,
It can fill the Seven Seas
With infinity to Spare.

How *R*eaching is our Love,
There are not enough Stars in the Sky.

How *B*right is our Love,
Sun is but a Candle!

How *G*reat is our Love,
The very Galaxy is too small.

Our Love,
No Words,
No Deeds,
No Expressions
Say it better than
I Love You!

Word of Love

If only the words...
Could communicate what's in my heart.

Then you would know
How I Love You So.

Yet to this day
There is no Word
No Deeds

That says it better than
I Love You!!!

Daily Love

The rooster crows,
The Sun rises and peeks through the blinds
The dawn of a new day,
I cannot wait to say,
I love you.

High noon,
The day is at its peak,
It's time to show you
How much I love you.

Sun sets upon another day.
The night begins to shine.
Before this day passes,
I have to quickly whisper,
I love you!!

The Defense

The Ocean
Has Depth
Can you touch bottom?

The Cloud
Has Lighting
Bolts that level trees

A Rose
Has Thorns
To protect its beauty

A Turtle
Has its Shell
To keep from harm's way

A Lion
Has its Roar
Approach at your own risk

A Cheetah
Has Speed
Catch me if you can

An Elephant
Has Size
Mass over might

A Shark
Has Stealth
Striking fear and awe in one and all

But;
Our Love
Has God!

The Treasure

The Treasure
Sits in a Vault, more secure than Ft Knox.

The Vault
Encased in Concrete.
Concrete so thick,
Only God can measure.

Concrete
Placed within an iceberg
Added Security.

At the very door stands the Sentinel,
Angel of the Lord
Protecting
The Treasure.

The Treasure,
Some look to acquire,
To own,
To Steal,
What can only be given.

Yet,
One passed the Sentinel like the Wind.
Penetrated the ice like it was puddle.
Torn the Concrete like it was paper.
Cut the Vault like a knife through butter.

I look to the Sentinel
The sign is given.

To thee,
I give the Only Treasure I own
My Heart!!!

Treasured Moment

Since that very moment
It has been treasured!

Bronze, Silver, and Gold
Have no value
For that moment is priceless!

I have built a Shrine,
To that moment.
Forever is it engraved within my mind!
Forever is it itched in my heart!

Day after day
Year after Year
Only add more value to that Moment

I will always treasure
The Moment
That I first said;
I Love You!

Your Smile

I stare into your Eyes
Glazing upon the Beauty
Few can see!

I watch as the Sun shines
Magnifying your Beauty

I smile as the moon glows
Reflecting upon your Face.
How your Beauty robs me of words!

I give Thanks
As I see how the Lord has touched thee!

I give Thanks
For there are no other words!

Then as you turn
Your Smile lights the room

I began to reflect...

Upon the Words...

I Love You!!!

Forbidden Dream

A Word and Smile
Penetrates the mind
Again and again

Forbidden Dream
Entertaining thoughts
Love and Happiness
To death does us apart.

Forbidden Dream
Wipe your eyes, when you cry
Bring laughter, where there is sorrow
Pamper you…
To grant your wishes, dreams, and
    desires.

Forbidden Dream
To Love You …
Until Tomorrow…
A Tomorrow, which never arrives
To Love You
Timelessly
Endlessly
Completely

Forbidden Dream
To grow young together
Knowing that Today
Is more Loving that Yesterday!
And YESTERDAY,
Yesterday, yesterday was perfect!

Forbidden Dream
World says No
To you and I…

Forbidden Dream
How I wish
I was the one!

Forbidden Dream
A Toast,
To Friendship!
A Silent Toast,
To the Forbidden Dream,
My Love for You!

My Love for You

The beauty of a pearl
The polish of a diamond
The smell of a fresh cut rose
Treasured more than gold.
That's my love for you.

The setting of the Sun
The splendor of a moonlit evening
The majesty of the mountains
Calm of golden pond
That is my love for you.

Today I dream,
For words...
For expressions...
For ways to say,
I love you!

Expression of Love

My heart is sadden this day
For I cannot truly tell thee how much I love thee

A picture is worth a thousand words
Yet, a thousand pictures still not enough.

I evaluated every word known to man
Still there are no words
No expressions.

I gladly lay down my life for thee,
But even that is only a shallow expression of my love.

My love for thee is so great
There is nothing on earth available to express it.
My love for thee is second only to God's love for thee!

Another Expression of Love

I have searched from top to bottom,
From north to south

I have read countless books,
I viewed thousands of pictures,
Picked endless roses,
Still there is nothing to truly express my love for you.

I shower you with gifts.
I guard your every move.
Pray for your well being,
Still that is not enough.

I lay down my life for you,
Yet, that is still a small token of my love.

From this day forward,
Let it be known,
That only God loves you more than *I*!

Your Love is a Dream

Grace
Style
Elegance
I noticed the moment I saw you

Intelligence
Sincerity
Compassion
I noticed the moment you first spoke

Beauty belong the immigration
Smile befitting an angle
Patience of a Saint
You are more than any one person deserves

I stare
With disbelief

Your Walk
The way you Talk
Even how you comb your hair

You are a Dream come true

NO!

You are,
GOD's answer to my Prayer.

Love

To explain the unexplainable

There are no know Words
To explain my Love

There are no Deeds
To show my Love

For Death
Has no bound on my Love

For in a Finite World

The only explanation
Are the words

God, I Love You!!!